Light Verse for DARK DAYS

How to keep going when the going gets rough

by Spike the Chicken

Light Verse for **DARK DAYS**
by Spike the Chicken

© Bonnie Durrance, 2013. All rights reserved.
ISBN 978-0-578-12934-1
Published by Spike the Chicken Press

No part of this book may be used or reproduced in any manner whatsoever without written permission except in the case of reprints in the context of reviews.

Text and illustrations by Bonnie Durrance

Book design by John Bull

For information write:
SpikeTheChicken@gmail.com

To all those who have ever felt
buffeted by the whims of fate and
need a little hope to carry on.

And for those who are sticklers
for limerick exactitude –
I've taken liberties with the count,
but not the rhythm of the form.
If you don't believe me,
read them aloud!

Introduction

Depending on our outlook, each new day arrives on our doorstep like a gift – or like a ticking bomb. This little book is meant to help you unwrap the gift, even if things seem to be blowing apart all around you.

There are times when I wonder what I'm doing, how I'm going to get everything done, if what I've already done is fantastic or a mess, or if I'm really, truly on the right path. Sometimes, waiting for a call, or a check, or an answer to the meaning of it all, I feel my creativity could be crushed under the burden of daily life. In one such stressful phase, I decided to set some time each day to let my writing Muse go play. I settled on the limerick form because…it's just not possible to feel sorry for yourself while writing a limerick!

Day by day, I found the limericks were bringing me gifts that were helping me move me on to a new creative plane. I want to share the gifts with you. So I've put my favorites together with my drawings, and I am letting Spike the Chicken, my actual, living hen, whose zest for life is a constant joy, author this book. We both hope you enjoy it and maybe share it with a friend.

Bonnie Durrance, 2013

Help!

When the future is shrouded in fog

And I feel less like a wheel than a cog

I'm adrift in the ocean

I must stay in motion

God – if you can't send a boat, send a log!

Breathe

I feel like a climber, approaching the 'core'

Scared to look back – afraid to move fore

To get proper traction

I need interaction

Or, to hell with it – let go and soar.

Move

It takes courage to push past the breakers

They seem to stretch out for acres

Past the pounding and wailing

I know there's smooth sailing

The course is not mine, but my Maker's.

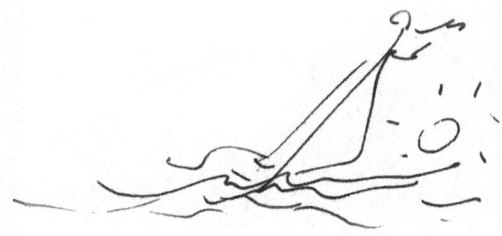

Reminder

If I think of this next stage as flight

It may help to remember that fright

Is a drag to the system

So blessings, let's list 'em

And fears will then vanish from sight.

Hiatus

Consider this phase a correction

A chance to alter direction

Just follow your bliss

Not bad advice, this

The point of it all is connection.

Driving

My father said, "Look, you always can steer!"

There's always a way – just not always clear

If on ice, you can slide

Turn the wheel to the side

Angels guide, if you're willing to hear.

Spring Cleaning

Transition invites a new start

Old patterns to be taken apart

Sort through all those

What doesn't work, goes!

Clearing out will be good for the heart.

New Horizons

Some days, having reached a plateau

Seems there's nowhere before me to go

I could go wash the dishes

Or follow my wishes

And sail away in a bright new bateau.

With or without Feathers

Today my thoughts turn to hope

As sort of a positive trope

It will take concentration

To let go expectation

It's a little like climbing a rope.

Panic wears many disguises

Like reluctance to face what arises

If I try to see through it

And relax and just do it

I'm up for whatever surprises.

Weight

Anxiety's like a big sack

Pressing down on your head and your back

Whatever's inside it

Grows worse when you hide it

Best to open it up and unpack.

Steps

Looking forward can make my heart sicken

Time is fleeting; I hear the clock tickin'

To succeed I must pause

Obey Nature's laws

Take one step at a time, like a chicken.

Remedy

When anxiety wakes you at three

Saying, Ha! And you thought you were free

Brush aside what you dread

That's just reared its head

And go make a nice cup of green tea.

Another Remedy

Today I face the temptation

To see life with a grim trepidation

But here's a confession

It's just an obsession

What I probably need's a vacation.

ANXIETY

Point of view

At night when my future is reeling

I seek answers high up in the ceiling

Beyond it, the sky

Below it, am I

The reminder is simple, but healing.

Mood

Dressed up in new crisis, what is this old pain?

I thought was resolved, but is now back again?

I hate to be rude

But perhaps it's a mood

Or the lowering pressure of oncoming rain.

Time

Some days when I haven't a minute

Can't stitch it – will just have to pin it

I just have to pause

It's important because

I could miss my whole life, while I'm in it.

Clarity

Sometimes a veil comes over my eyes

Portraying events in odd shapes and size

It's easy to shift it

Let Nature lift it

Sometimes pain is a gift in disguise.

Rain

When it rains it sometimes will pour

And each problem seems followed by more

It can drive you to tears

But let not your fears

Be a drag on your little boat's oar.

Attitude Adjustment

If necessity mothers invention

And creativity counters convention

Then I think it is great

Though I've come to it late

To see challenge with thanks, not contention.

Calm

Imagine your fears have no basis

And the cards in your hand are all Aces

Then emotions and brain

Can get on the same train

I think the term for it is homeostasis.

Embracing Adversity

The rain has been pounding my roses

They're bowed down in dispirited poses

But like crises I know

The rain helps them grow

Sometimes gifts are right under our noses.

Antidote

I saw a woman who looked up and said

"Some days I don't want to get out of bed."

With house under water

The economy's got her

I said, try to be grateful instead.

Cultivation

Scanning the field of my needs

I must separate flowers from weeds

And adjust my ambition

Improve my condition

And see outreach as scattering seeds.

Prayer

When routine is taken away

And you're unsure of your purpose each day

While it's not about kneeling

I do find it's healing

To turn inward and learn how to pray.

Make your Own Reality

To get what you want, they say you should dream

Picture the coffee and here comes the cream

But I've learned growing flowers

Success comes with showers

And help from a being Supreme.

Reminder

This morning I thought I would mention

Creativity loves reinvention

And refuses the blues

That often ensues

When money confuses intention.

Sunday

On Sunday this chicken sleeps late

Says she's got too much now on her plate

With calendar freed up

Time seems to speed up

And with it the need to create.

Challenge

There's nothing quite like an assignment

To get rid of the sense of confinement

When writing a tome

All alone and at home

To give me and my Muse new alignment.

Block

Today, my mind is a blank
I've used up all thoughts in the tank
When creativity drains
It's like land without rains
The wise keep reserves in the bank.

Fame

Oscars acknowledge the best

Inspiration they give to the rest

Do your work well

Your reward – who can tell?

It's in the doing we're blessed.

Mindset

Climbing molehills or mountains

the same rules apply

You must wake up and get dressed

and go out and try

So get out of bed

And walk straight ahead

You can rest long enough when you die.

Practice

I heard someone practicing flute

She barely could manage a toot

She sounded so terrible

But to give up – unbearable

Love the practice, the outcome is moot.

Puzzlement

Sometimes effort is like a Zen koan

Or as Sisyphus said of the stone

As I push it uphill

I learn about will

How surrender's reward all its own.

MARKETPLACE

Anything But That

These days the economy's tanking

CEOs have been given a spanking

While they get impunity

I'm for new opportunity

Just not a career in banking.

Prediction

My Gemini horoscope says, "This

Is the year for professional bliss"

Sure hope it's true

And wealth will accrue

Debt is something I'm not going to miss.

Visualization

Designing a job is a task

For those willing to work and to ask

What's the best I can do?

Who's the boss, me or you?

You want me or a corporate mask?

Progress

When laid off, I feared I'd be poor

Reading Want Ads, oh God, what a bore!

But now I'm in motion

Like a sloop on the ocean

Soon I'll be better by far than before.

Still Seeking Work

Looking out at the wide open roads

While the economy grimly ill bodes

I take stock of my assets

All the skills and the facets

Doors will open if I just know the codes.

Survival

When money and soul are at odds

And I'm tearing my hair out in wads

It helps to divide

What's out from inside

Give Caesar what's Caesar's and God what is God's.

How Stimulus Works

So, I've almost no money at all

I said, going into the Mall

But in the new Apple Store

Came the faith I'd earn more

I went smiling away with my haul.

Relief

At last, Unemployment's okayed me

I fear my relief has betrayed me

I say money's no issue

But hand me a tissue

I'll stop crying as soon as they've paid me!

Focus

When the weather is clear, bright and sunny

Way too nice to be dwelling on money

Take a tip from a flower

Who counts life by the hour

Taste the moment – it's all milk and honey.

Side Effects

Last night, we turned forward the clocks

I'd like to save that lost hour in a box

But for now I don't need it

Because time – I don't heed it

For the lazy, unemployment rocks.

Choice

In the fields all the flowers are blooming

On CNN – a depression is looming

Call it denial

I'm switching the dial

To the birds, the economy's booming.

Wise Advice

This morning I took a friend's hint
Too much worry gives life a dull tint
For a day I may shirk
All this looking for work
It's a marathon, right? Not a sprint.

Providence

When pondering how to stay viable

To the laid off, most anything's try-able

Put out a jam stand

Start up a rock band

Grace is – when you trust it – reliable.

Time to Play

Orangutans swing through the trees

Butterflies dance with the bees

The laid off are snoozing

It's no pay they are losing

Ah! The time unemployment frees!

Pitfalls

A job has a schedule I never like – but

Its demands get me out of habitual rut

With proper incentive

On my own, I'm inventive

But if it's not done today then, so what?

Priorities

A boyfriend I saw once at noon

When I said, "Must get back to work soon"

Replied, "I'm all for shirking

You miss so much when working"

Such a sweet unemployment tune!

Letting go

My view of the future is now more benign

Suddenly freed from a boss's design

I'll get off the divan

And go do what I can

Which will be what my Muse will define.

Happiness

Cloud Lifter

It's so often said it's a platitude

That happiness springs from one's attitude

When the future looks scary

Advice to the wary

Is – every day practice your gratitude.

Opposition

In summer, we long for cool air

When standing, we'd rather a chair

What we long for is not

Whatever we've got

I'd say being human's a bear.

Lighten Up

In ambiguous times, the wise person knows

That certainty is but an optimist's pose

You may cling to belief

If it gives you relief

But the happy take life as it goes.

Freedom

Imagine a life without things

And the tension that wealth often brings

It can make a heart harden

Better play in the garden

Just step into it and the mind sings.

Expansion

When I was younger my worst fear was that

No matter how thin, I was sure I looked fat

Now older and wise

I'm at home in my size

Life's a banquet I'm glad that I'm at.

Dream

Today someone asked me if I had a dream

Like making film of a river or stream

I replied, "Sure…

But the way is not clear…"

She said, "Obstacles aren't what they seem."

Spring

After sleeping, my problems are few

I wake up alert – but not too

Spring is arriving

The green grass is thriving

Makes me want to go nap in the dew.

Living Simply

The life of the chicken is deceptively sweet

Peck on each other. Get something to eat.

They heed not tomorrow

Beg not nor borrow

Their day in itself is complete.

Respite

Sunday's for rest, the Creator decreed

For those work obsessed, it's what we need

No obligations

No guilt or negations

Give thanks and go do a good deed.

Wealth

Consider our value is tallied in gold

Not the kind you invest in, to keep or be sold

But what glints through the trees

And shines on the breeze

And can grow with you as you get old.

Paradox

Say you don't want something taken away

Whether burden or gift, who can say?

But with open hand, willing

You're a step toward fulfilling

Your destiny's plan for the day.

Essentials

In the vineyard a laborer's song
Said nothing in life could go wrong
He may own less than me
But his song helped me see
I've possessed what I sought all along.

Love

If you feel you're about at wits' end

Go take care of an animal friend

Feathered or furred

I give you my word

Love heals and we love what we tend.

Observation

Whoever's not had the blues
And felt stirred by some need to accuse
Seems we blame to feel stronger
Till the trick works no longer
And we have to relinquish our ruse.

Contentment

The toes of the chicken touch ground

With reverence, not making a sound

She snaps up a bug

Pulls a worm with a tug

Simple pleasures she finds all around.

Awakening

If there's somebody you wish to be

Or some mirror face you'd rather see

Take the wish from the shelf

Start the change in yourself

Once a day, just let yourself be.

Secret of Happiness

Consider the ceiling a tabula rasa

Where dreaming can take you from Napa to Llasa

So now – let me see

Just where should I be?

I think truly, right here en mi casa.

www.ingramcontent.com/pod-product-compliance
Lightning Source LLC
LaVergne TN
LVHW051155080426
835508LV00021B/2648